brass instruments repertoires

SUNAO ISAJI

POPONDETTA RAINBOW

for Trombone and Piano

伊左治 直

虹のポポンデッタ

トロンボーンとピアノのために

zen-on music

POPONDETTA RAINBOW for Trombone and Piano

When I work on a new composition, I sometimes get an idea from the shape of an instrument. The inside form of the grand piano, which produces rich sound, gave me an image of clear water in river or sea. And the trombone's shape made me visualize a fish swaying in the beautiful current of the sound. I overlaid the two images on each other. Therefore, the piano is used not only for creating its own sound but also for resonating the trombone's sound, by pressing the sustain pedal.

Popondetta Rainbow is the name of a tropical fish. The word Popondetta, which is the name of a city in Papua New Guinea, has a pleasant sound in itself. When the rainbow appears over the word, it becomes the name of a beautiful tropical fish that has subtle and watery colors. I was affected so much when I knew it. The impression is reflected on this work. Although Popondetta Rainbow is a proper noun, I translated the word rainbow into Japanese for the Japanese title, Niji no Popondetta.

Sunao ISAJI

Commissioned by Yoshiki Hakoyama

The world premiere(Recording) : June 27, 2012, at Katsushika Symphony Hills Iris Hall

Yoshiki Hakoyama (Trombone), Hitomi Takara (Piano)

Duration : approximately 6 minutes 30 seconds

CD : B-Music/BMCD-2002

虹のポポンデッタ　　トロンボーンとピアノのために

私は作曲に際して、楽器の形状から着想を得ることがあります。豊かな音響がある、グランドピアノの内部に川や海の澄んだ水中をイメージしたことから、トロンボーンには、その豊かな響きの中を揺蕩う魚の姿を、まず重ね合わせました。したがって、ピアノは演奏される「発音楽器」のみならず、ペダルを解放し、トロンボーンのソロを響かせる「共鳴楽器」としての意味も持っています。

ポポンデッタ・レインボーは熱帯魚の名前です。この「ポポンデッタ」（パプアニューギニアの地名）という言葉そのものの心地よい響き、そして、その語に「虹」が架かることで、かくも透き通った淡い色彩の、美しい熱帯魚の名前になることに、私は感動をおぼえました。そのことは作品に強く反映されていると思います。そのため邦題は敢えて、レインボーを日本語になおし「虹のポポンデッタ」としました。

伊左治 直

委嘱：箱山芳樹
録音初演：2012年6月27日、かつしかシンフォニーヒルズ・アイリスホール
　　　　　箱山芳樹（トロンボーン）、高良仁美（ピアノ）
演奏所要時間：約6分30秒
CD：「トロンボーン小品集」（B-Music／BMCD-2002）

POPONDETTA RAINBOW

for Trombone and Piano

Sunao ISAJI

POPONDETTA RAINBOW
for Trombone and Piano

Sunao ISAJI

10

伊左治 直 :虹のポポンデッタ ●

作曲─────────────────────伊左治　直
第1版第1刷発行──────────────2012年11月15日
発行───────────────────株式会社全音楽譜出版社
─────────────────────東京都新宿区上落合2丁目13番3号 〒161-0034
─────────────────────TEL・営業部 03・3227-6270
─────────────────────　　　　出版部 03・3227-6280
─────────────────────URL　http://www.zen-on.co.jp/
─────────────────────ISBN978-4-11-580016-8

複写・複製・転載等厳禁　Printed in Japan

12110126